THE BRAVE MAGELLAN
THE FIRST MAN TO CIRCUMNAVIGATE THE WORLD
Biography 3rd Grade
Children's Biography Books

Speedy Publishing LLC
40 E. Main St. #1156
Newark, DE 19711
www.speedypublishing.com

Ferdinand Magellan was an explorer who was born 1480 in Portugal and he died in Cebu, Philippines on April 27, 1521.

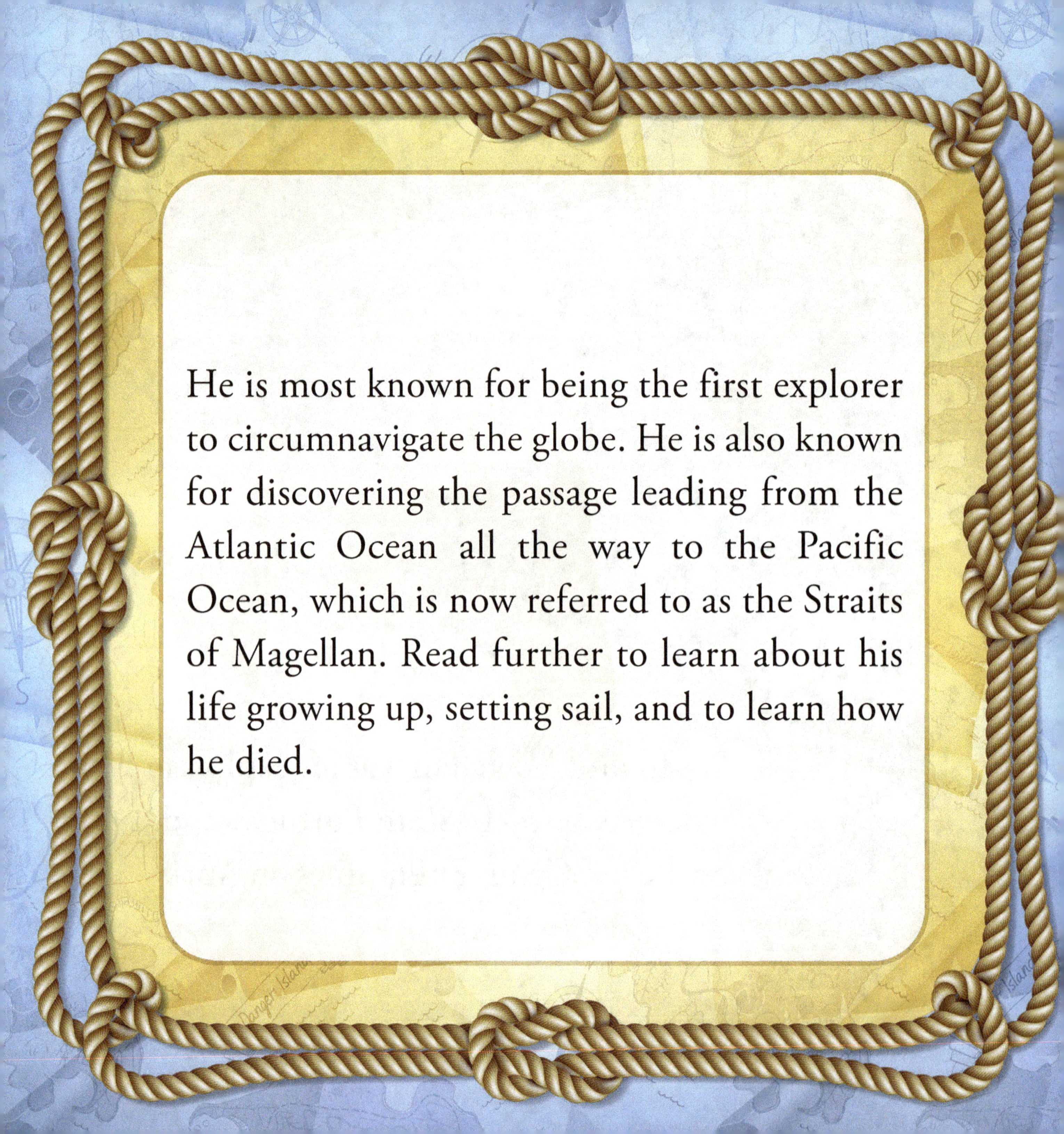

He is most known for being the first explorer to circumnavigate the globe. He is also known for discovering the passage leading from the Atlantic Ocean all the way to the Pacific Ocean, which is now referred to as the Straits of Magellan. Read further to learn about his life growing up, setting sail, and to learn how he died.

Strait of Magellan

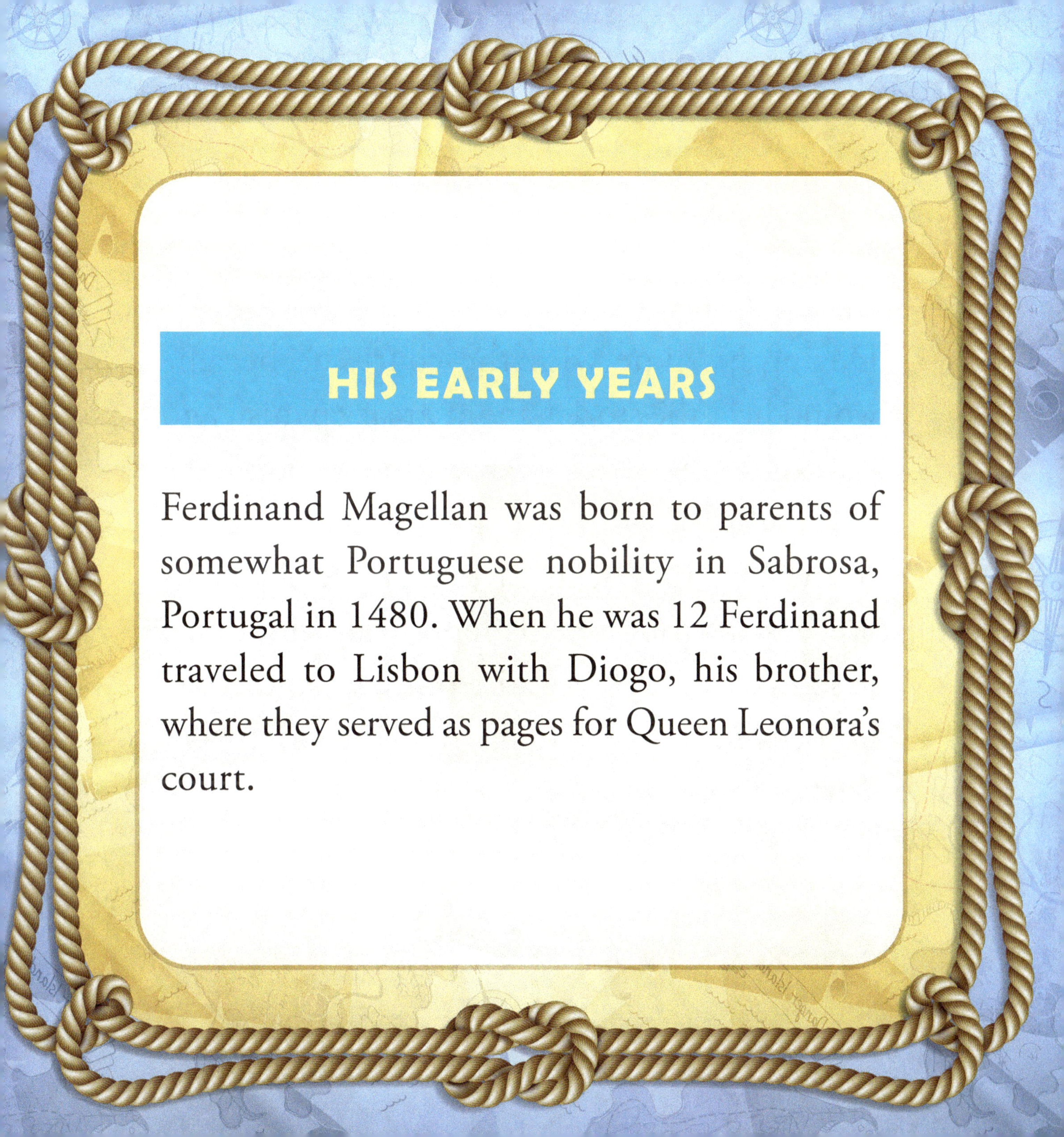

HIS EARLY YEARS

Ferdinand Magellan was born to parents of somewhat Portuguese nobility in Sabrosa, Portugal in 1480. When he was 12 Ferdinand traveled to Lisbon with Diogo, his brother, where they served as pages for Queen Leonora's court.

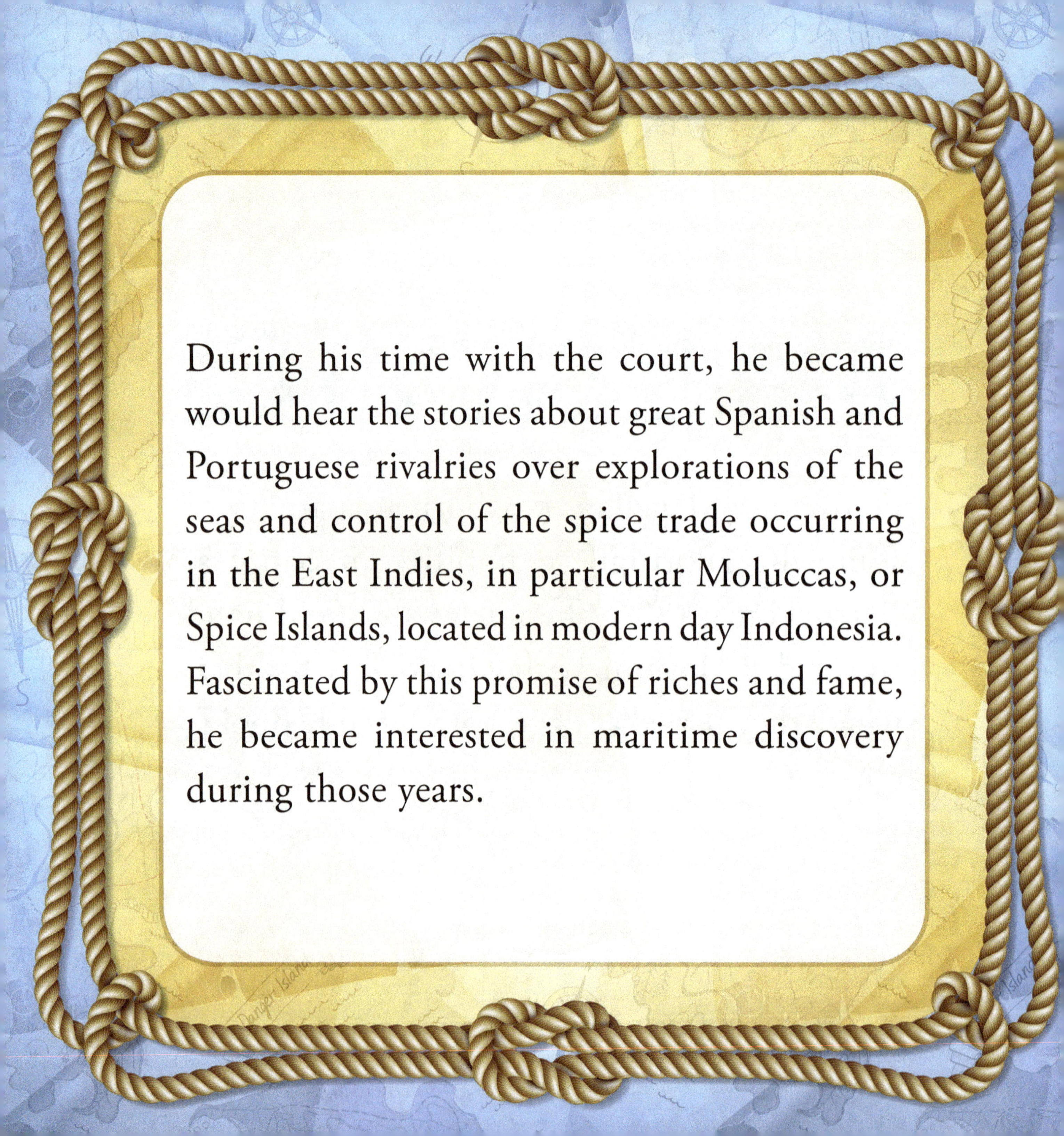

During his time with the court, he became would hear the stories about great Spanish and Portuguese rivalries over explorations of the seas and control of the spice trade occurring in the East Indies, in particular Moluccas, or Spice Islands, located in modern day Indonesia. Fascinated by this promise of riches and fame, he became interested in maritime discovery during those years.

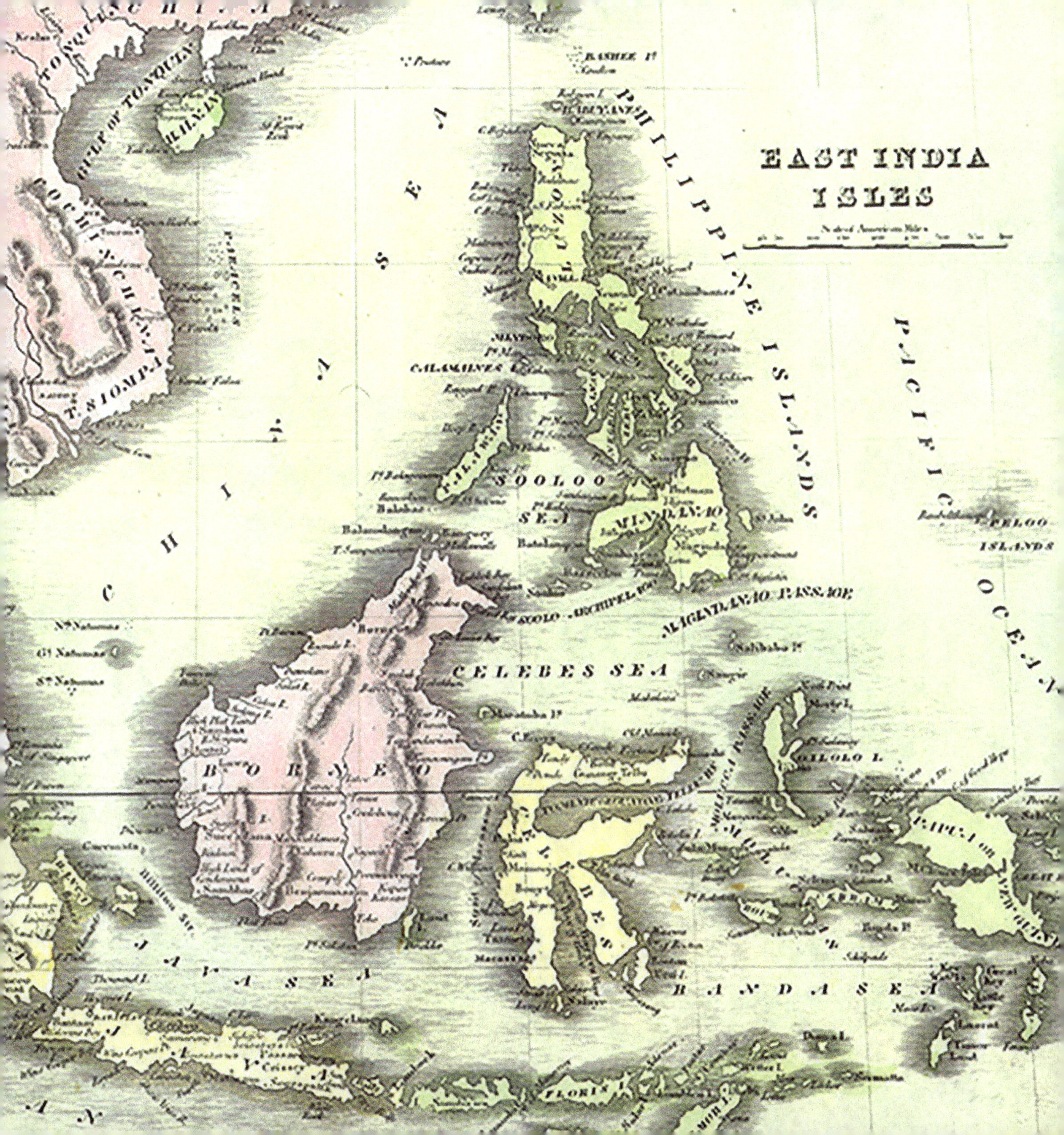

EAST INDIA
ISLES
PHILIPPINE ISLANDS
PACIFIC OCEAN
CHINA SEA
GULF OF TONQUIN
COCHIN CHINA
SOOLOO SEA
MINDANAO
CELEBES SEA
BORNEO
CELEBES
GILOLO I.
BANDA SEA
JAVA SEA
PELOO ISLANDS
SOOLO ARCHIPELAGO
MAGINDANAO PASSAGE
MOLUCCA PASSAGE
CALAMAINES
PALAWAN
SAMAR
BASHEE Is.

TIERRA DEL
FUEGO

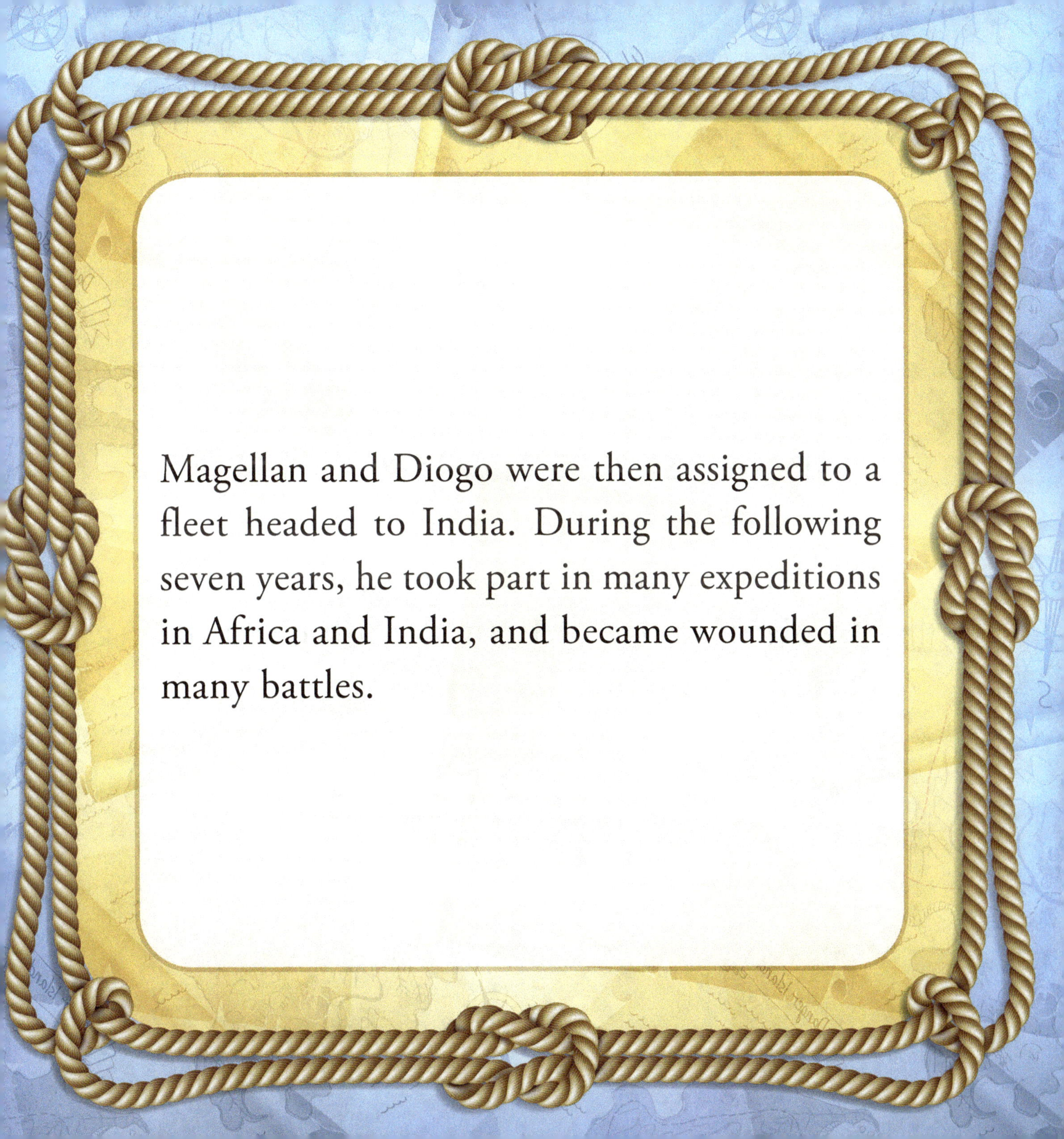

Magellan and Diogo were then assigned to a fleet headed to India. During the following seven years, he took part in many expeditions in Africa and India, and became wounded in many battles.

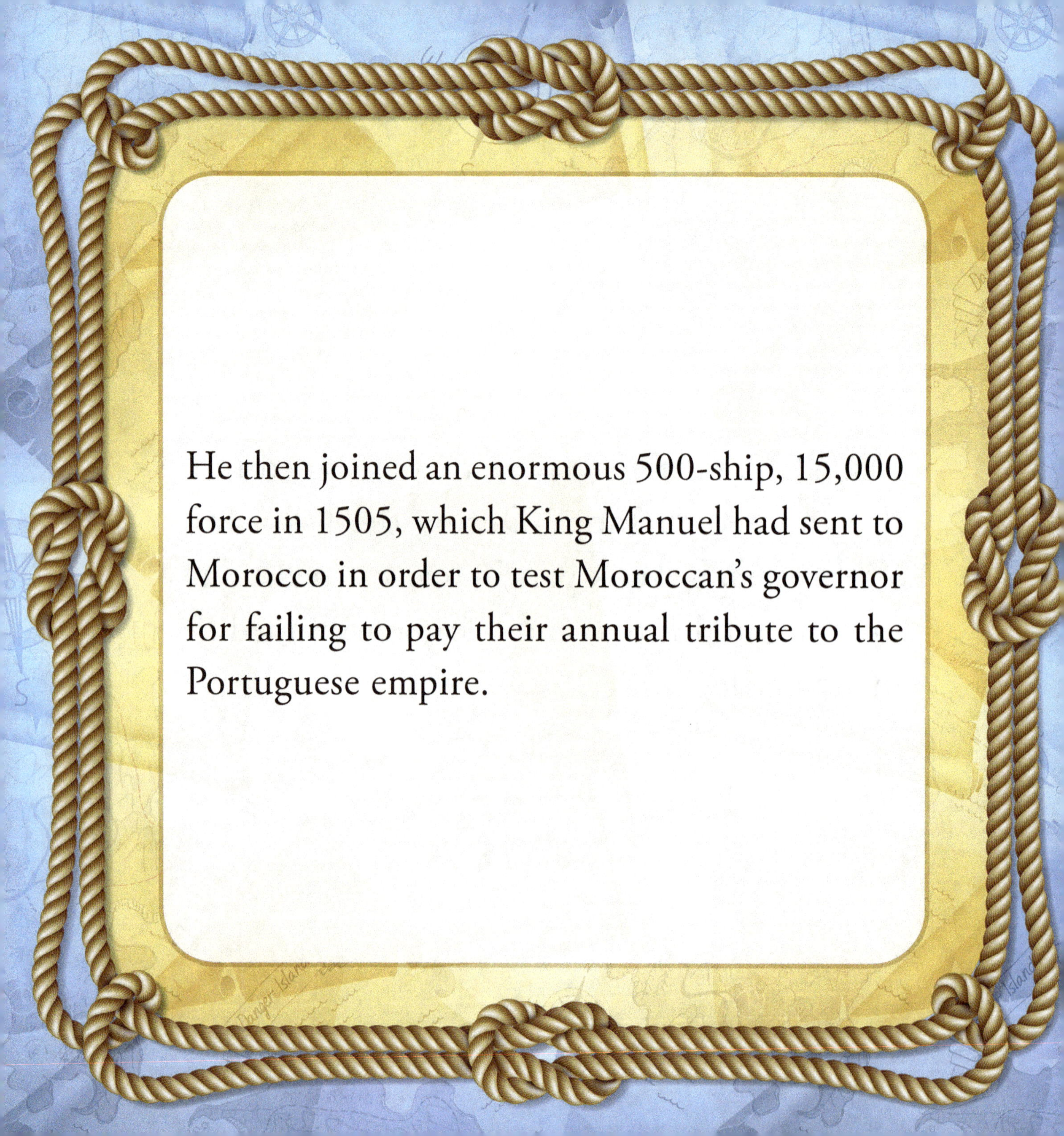

He then joined an enormous 500-ship, 15,000 force in 1505, which King Manuel had sent to Morocco in order to test Moroccan's governor for failing to pay their annual tribute to the Portuguese empire.

King Manuel

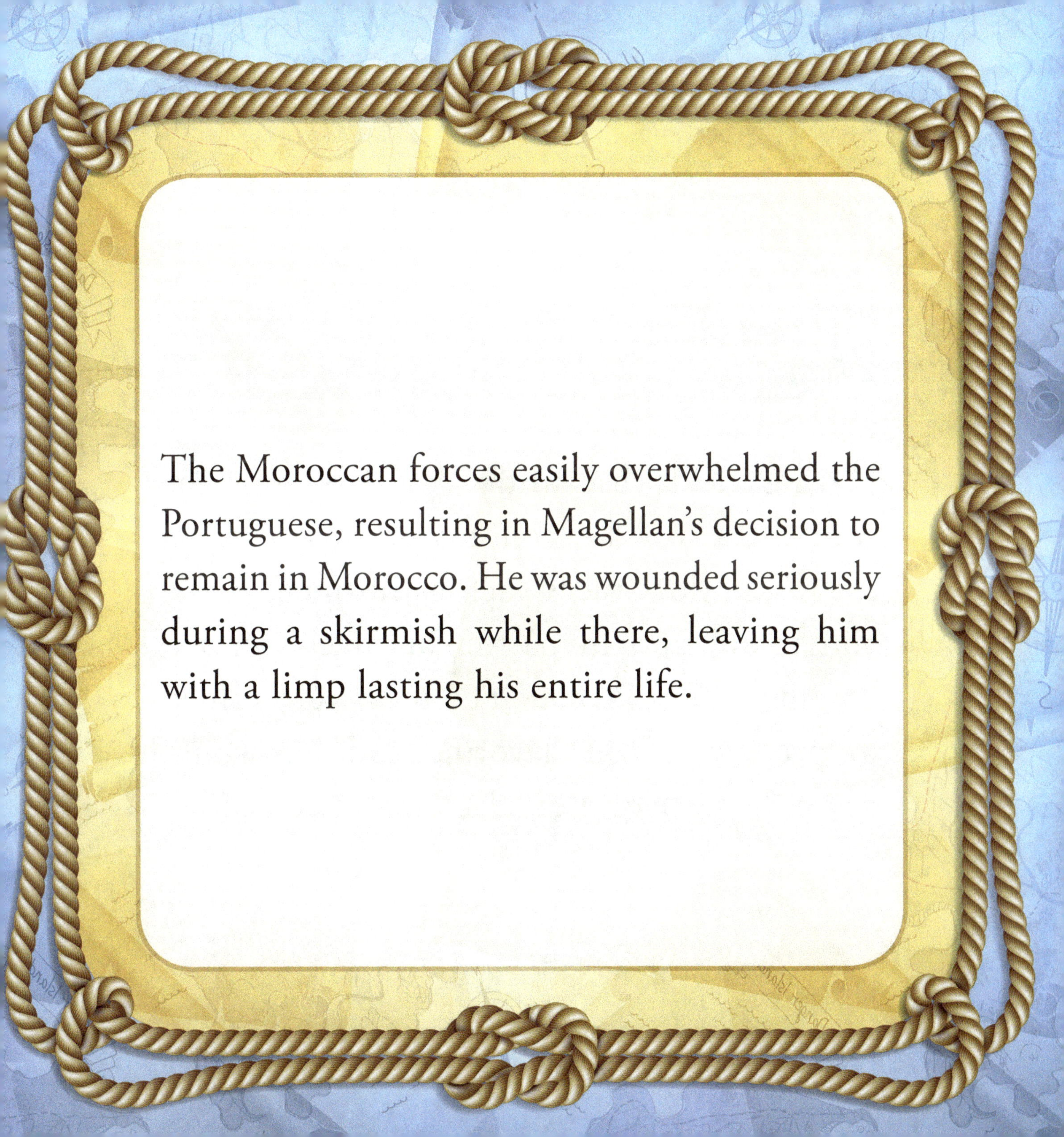

The Moroccan forces easily overwhelmed the Portuguese, resulting in Magellan's decision to remain in Morocco. He was wounded seriously during a skirmish while there, leaving him with a limp lasting his entire life.

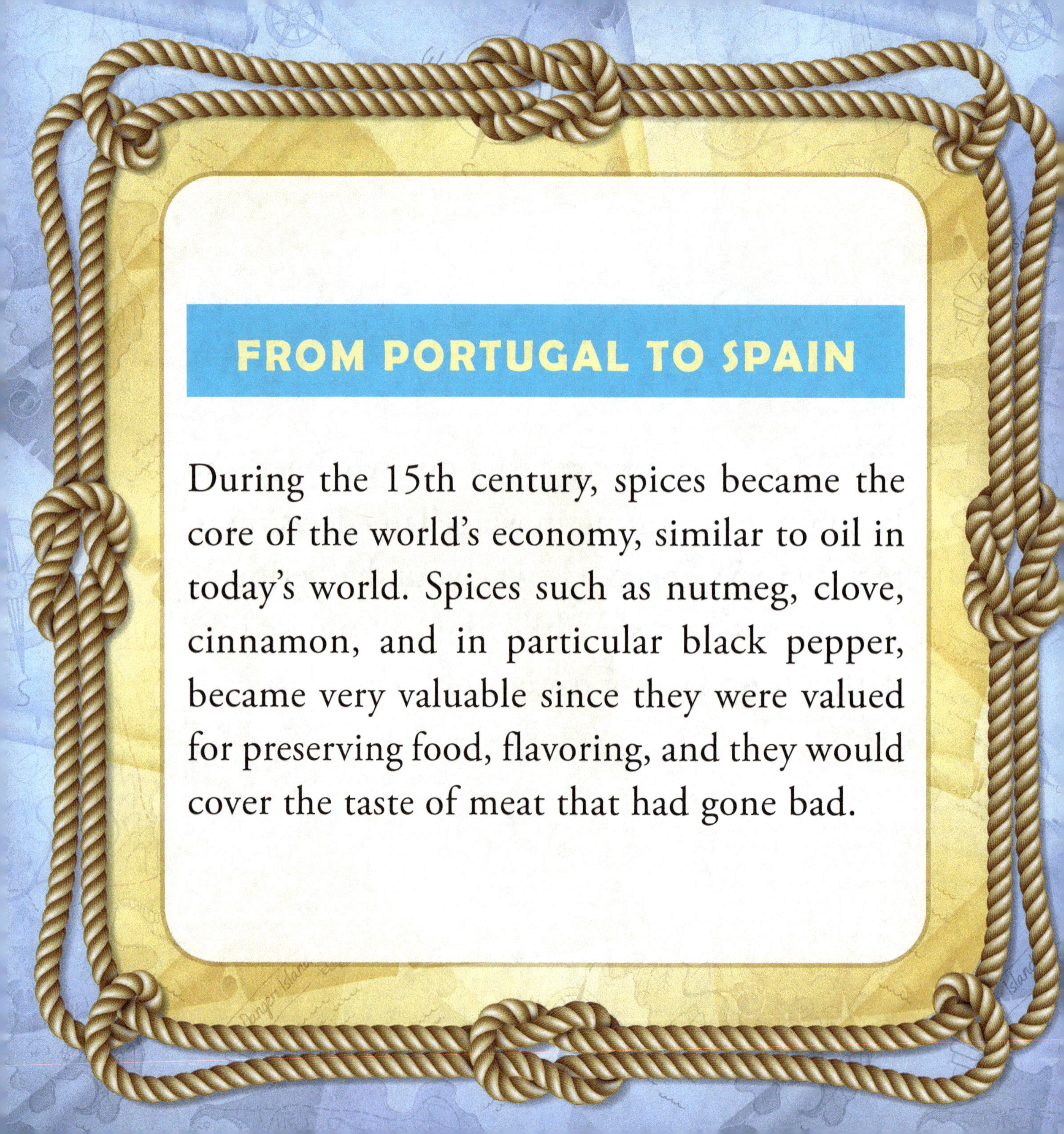

FROM PORTUGAL TO SPAIN

During the 15th century, spices became the core of the world's economy, similar to oil in today's world. Spices such as nutmeg, clove, cinnamon, and in particular black pepper, became very valuable since they were valued for preserving food, flavoring, and they would cover the taste of meat that had gone bad.

Strait of Magellan

Map of the Spice Islands
Morotai
Halmahera
Tidore
Maluku
Bacan
Sula
Obi
Misool
Seram
Buru
Ambon
Seram
Laut
Watebela
Banda
Maluku
Kai
Wetar
Babar
Leti
Tanimbar

Since they were not cultivated in the arid and cold Europe atmosphere, they had to find ways to find out the quickest way to get to the Spice Islands by sea.

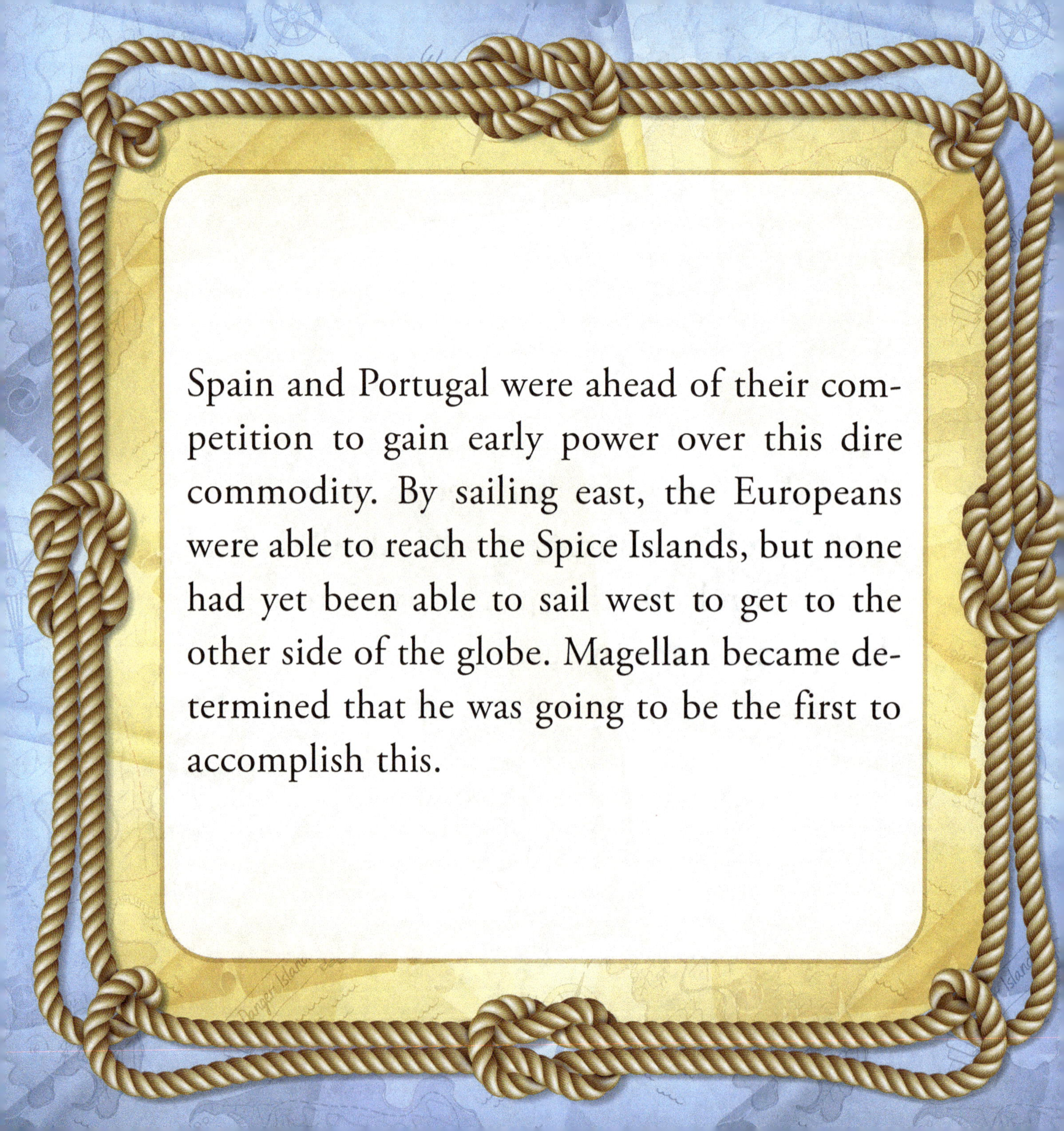

Spain and Portugal were ahead of their competition to gain early power over this dire commodity. By sailing east, the Europeans were able to reach the Spice Islands, but none had yet been able to sail west to get to the other side of the globe. Magellan became determined that he was going to be the first to accomplish this.

Victoria Ship

By this time, he had become a skilled seaman and he contacted Portugal's King Manuel seeking support for his voyage westward to these islands.

His request was refused repeatedly. He became frustrated and in 1517 he relinquished his nationality and moved to Spain seeking support of its royals for his venture.

Diogo Barbosa

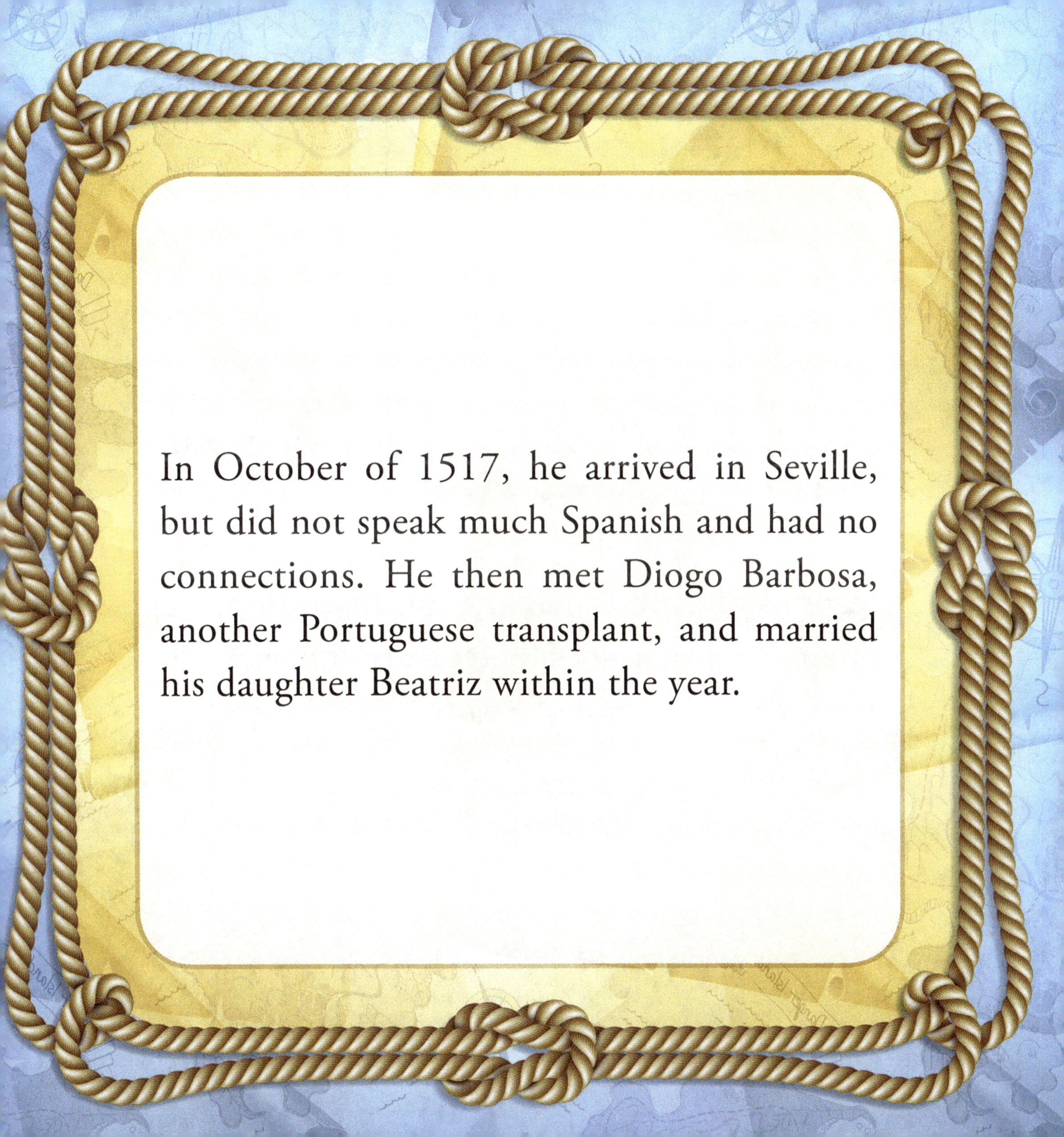

In October of 1517, he arrived in Seville, but did not speak much Spanish and had no connections. He then met Diogo Barbosa, another Portuguese transplant, and married his daughter Beatriz within the year.

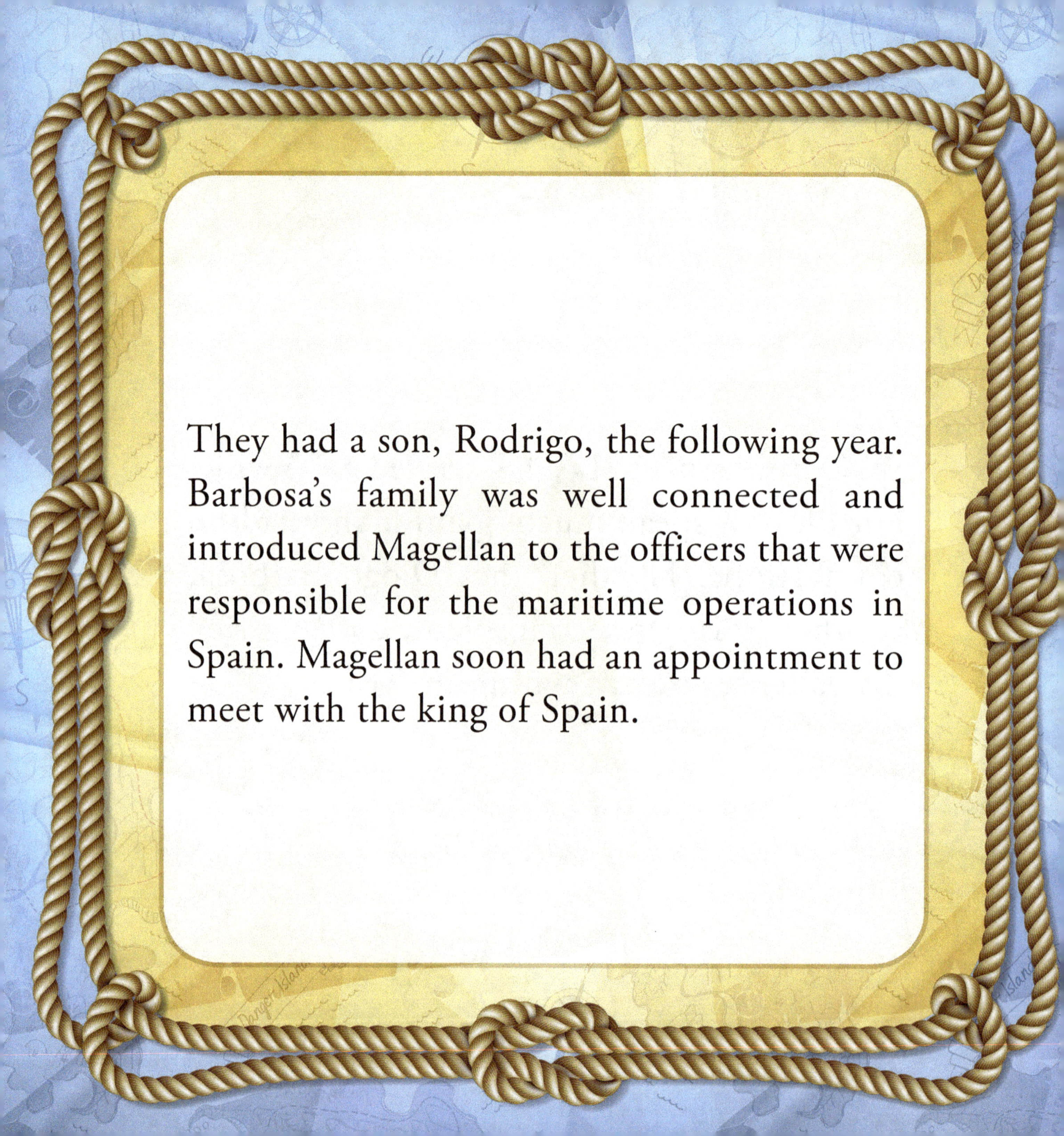

They had a son, Rodrigo, the following year. Barbosa's family was well connected and introduced Magellan to the officers that were responsible for the maritime operations in Spain. Magellan soon had an appointment to meet with the king of Spain.

King Charles of Spain

Queen Isabella

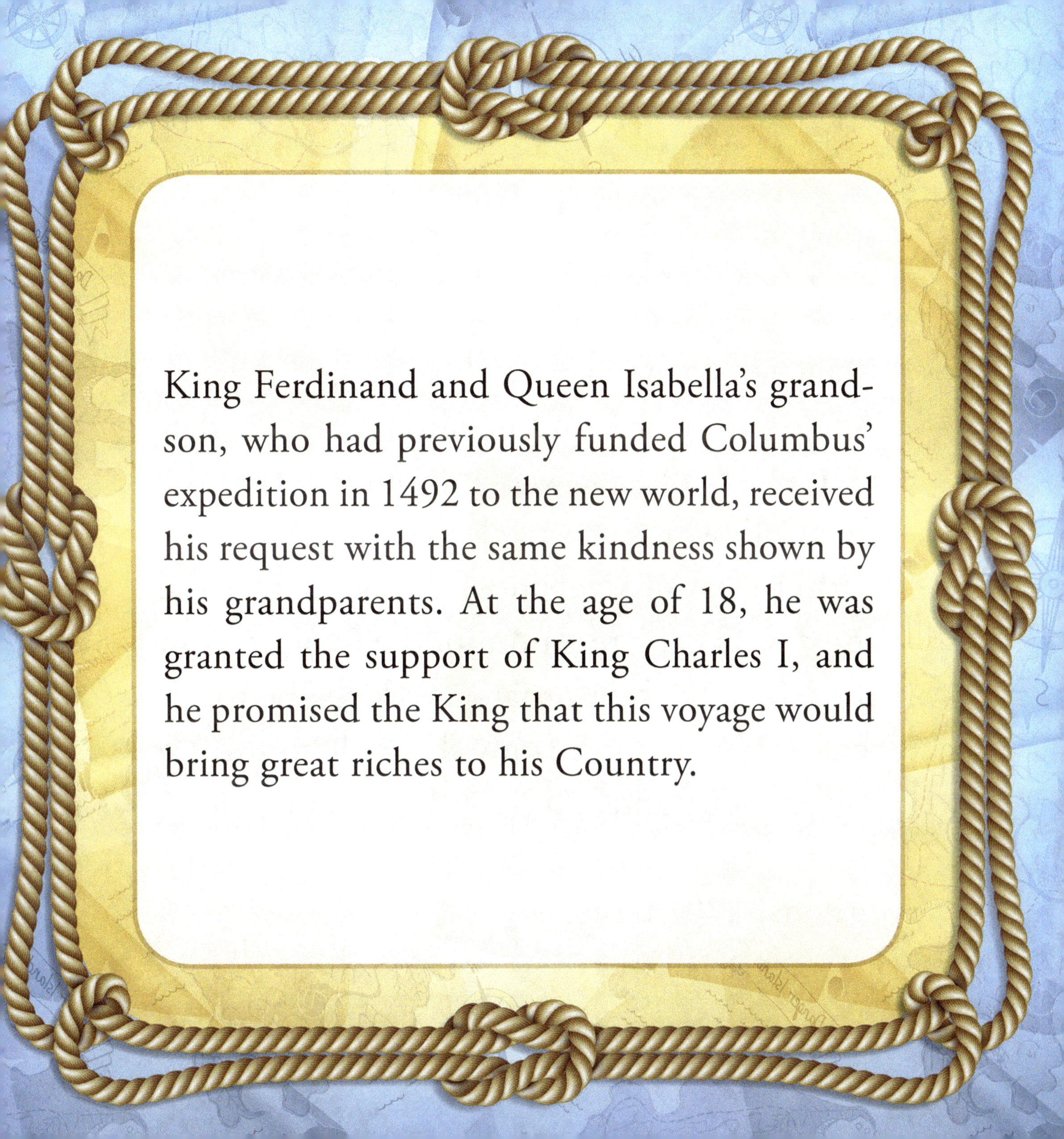

King Ferdinand and Queen Isabella's grandson, who had previously funded Columbus' expedition in 1492 to the new world, received his request with the same kindness shown by his grandparents. At the age of 18, he was granted the support of King Charles I, and he promised the King that this voyage would bring great riches to his Country.

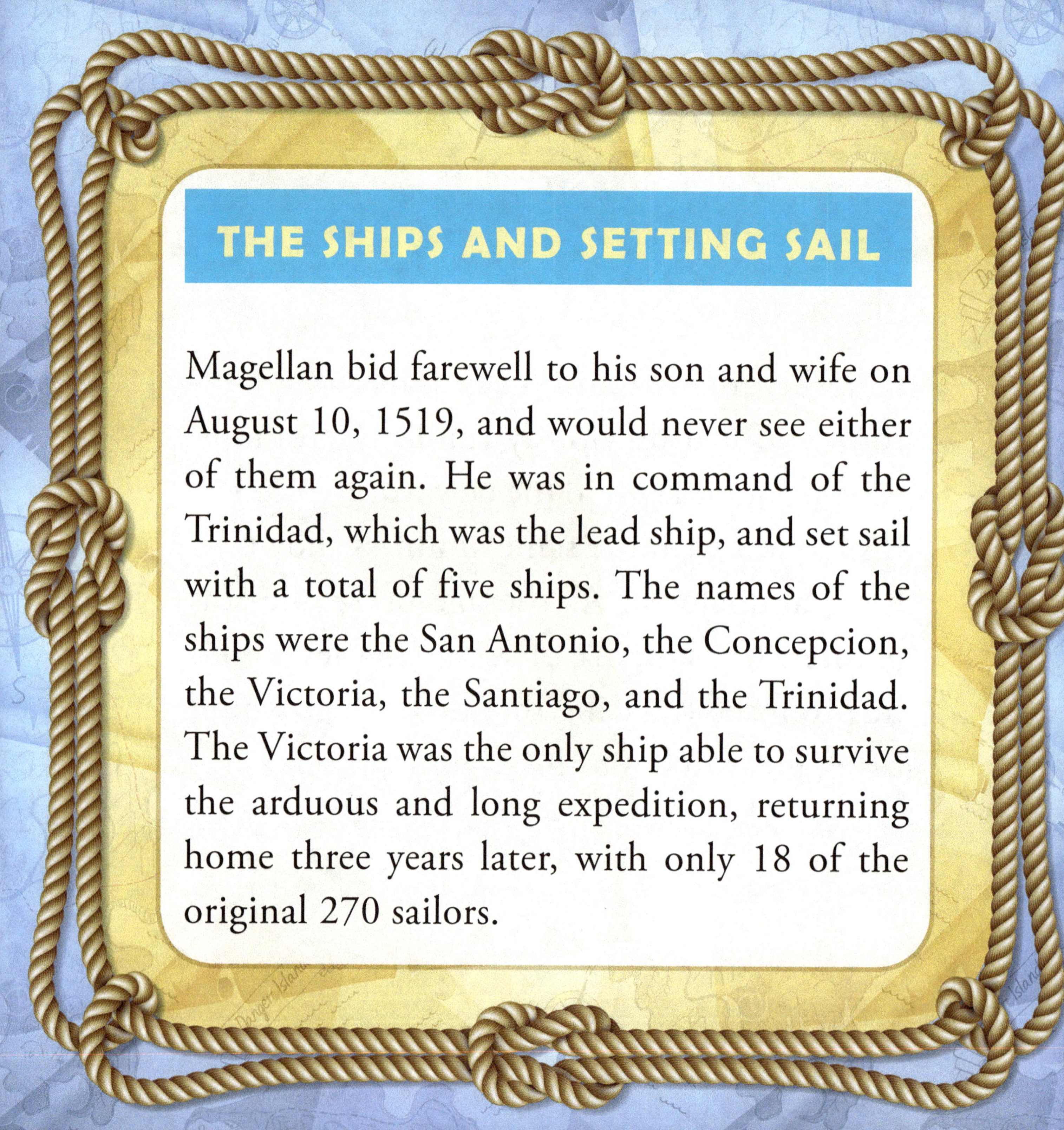

THE SHIPS AND SETTING SAIL

Magellan bid farewell to his son and wife on August 10, 1519, and would never see either of them again. He was in command of the Trinidad, which was the lead ship, and set sail with a total of five ships. The names of the ships were the San Antonio, the Concepcion, the Victoria, the Santiago, and the Trinidad. The Victoria was the only ship able to survive the arduous and long expedition, returning home three years later, with only 18 of the original 270 sailors.

Victoria

Port San Julian

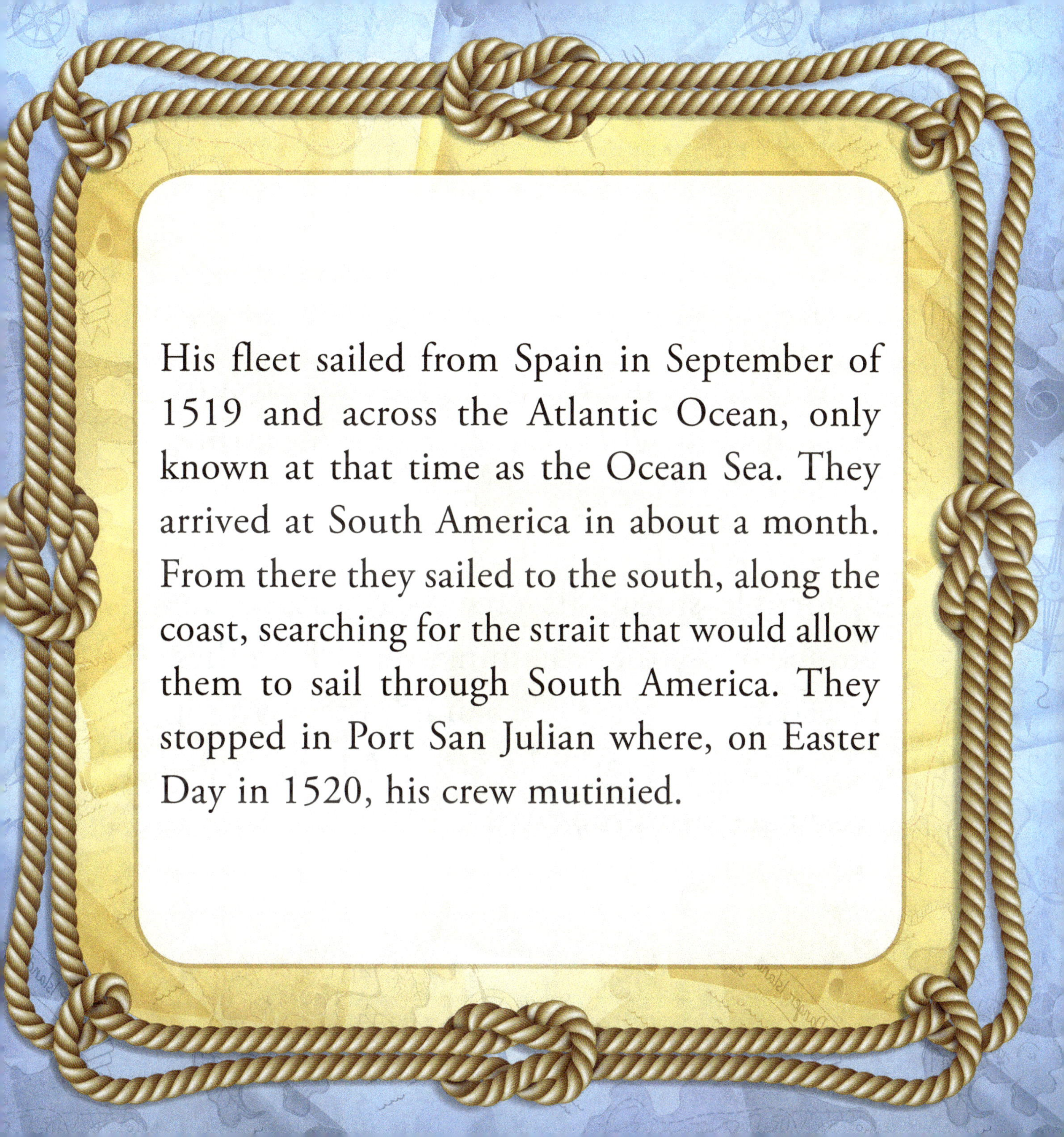

His fleet sailed from Spain in September of 1519 and across the Atlantic Ocean, only known at that time as the Ocean Sea. They arrived at South America in about a month. From there they sailed to the south, along the coast, searching for the strait that would allow them to sail through South America. They stopped in Port San Julian where, on Easter Day in 1520, his crew mutinied.

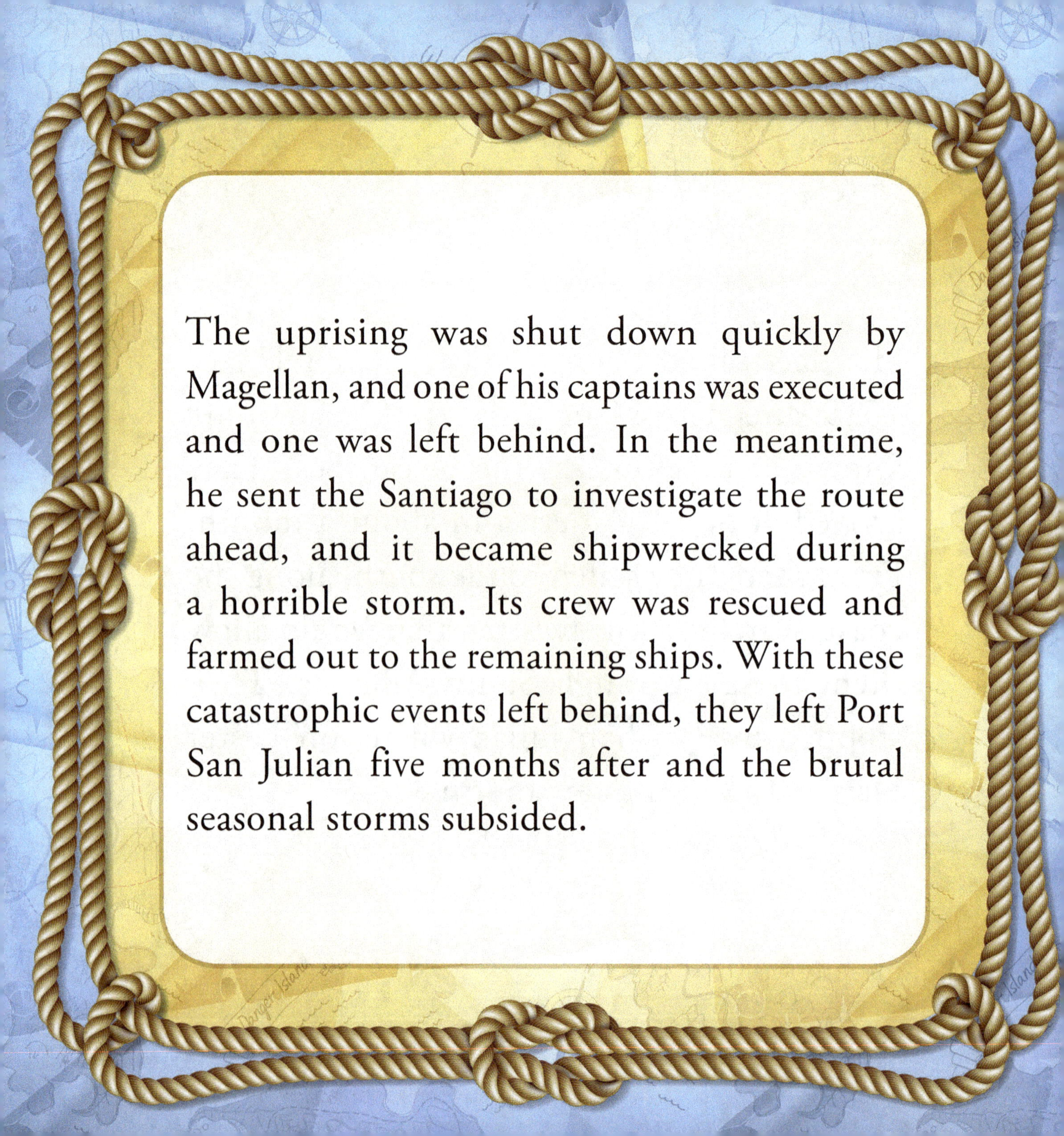

The uprising was shut down quickly by Magellan, and one of his captains was executed and one was left behind. In the meantime, he sent the Santiago to investigate the route ahead, and it became shipwrecked during a horrible storm. Its crew was rescued and farmed out to the remaining ships. With these catastrophic events left behind, they left Port San Julian five months after and the brutal seasonal storms subsided.

HERNANDO DE MAGALLANES

Strait of Magellan

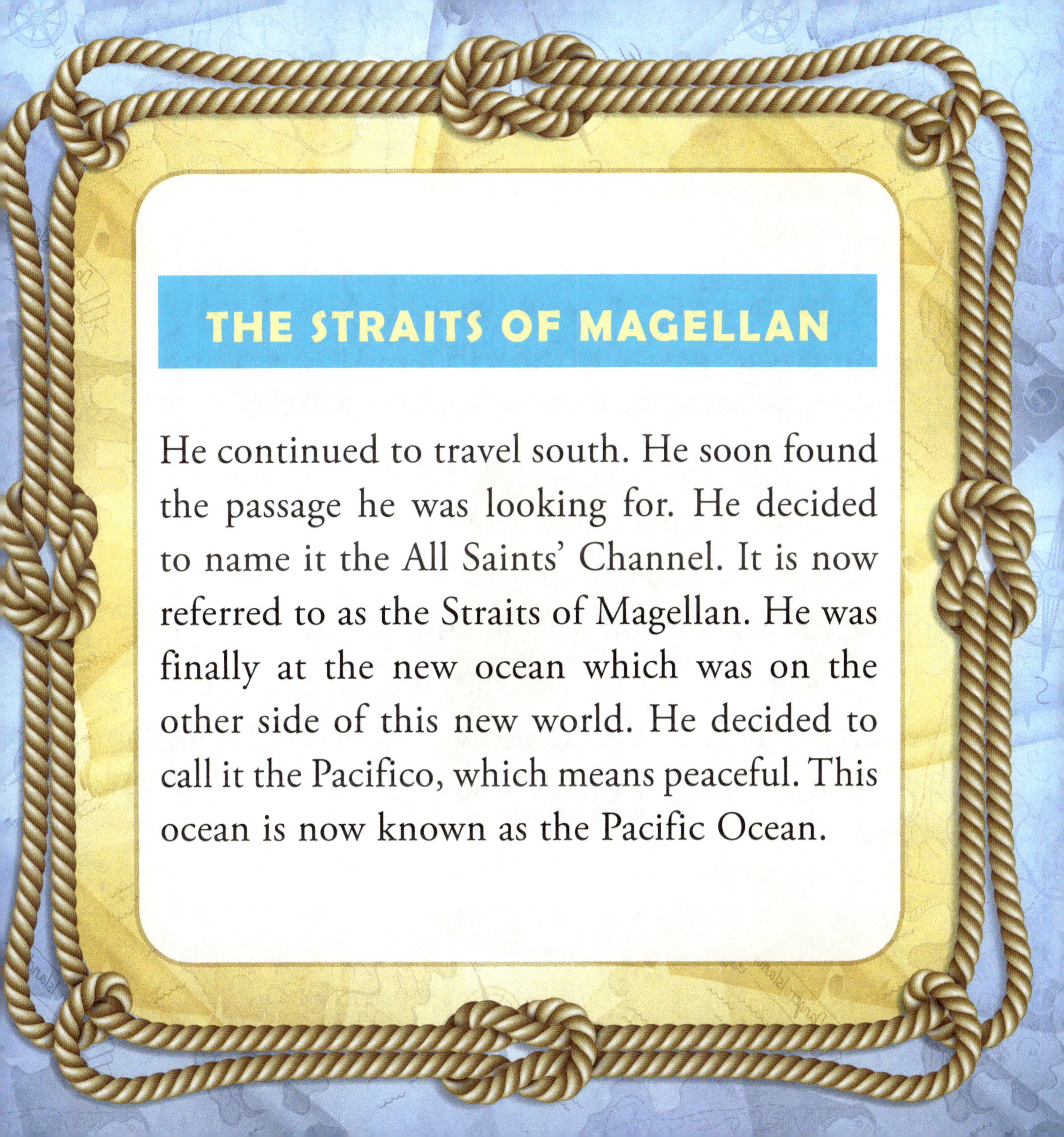

THE STRAITS OF MAGELLAN

He continued to travel south. He soon found the passage he was looking for. He decided to name it the All Saints' Channel. It is now referred to as the Straits of Magellan. He was finally at the new ocean which was on the other side of this new world. He decided to call it the Pacifico, which means peaceful. This ocean is now known as the Pacific Ocean.

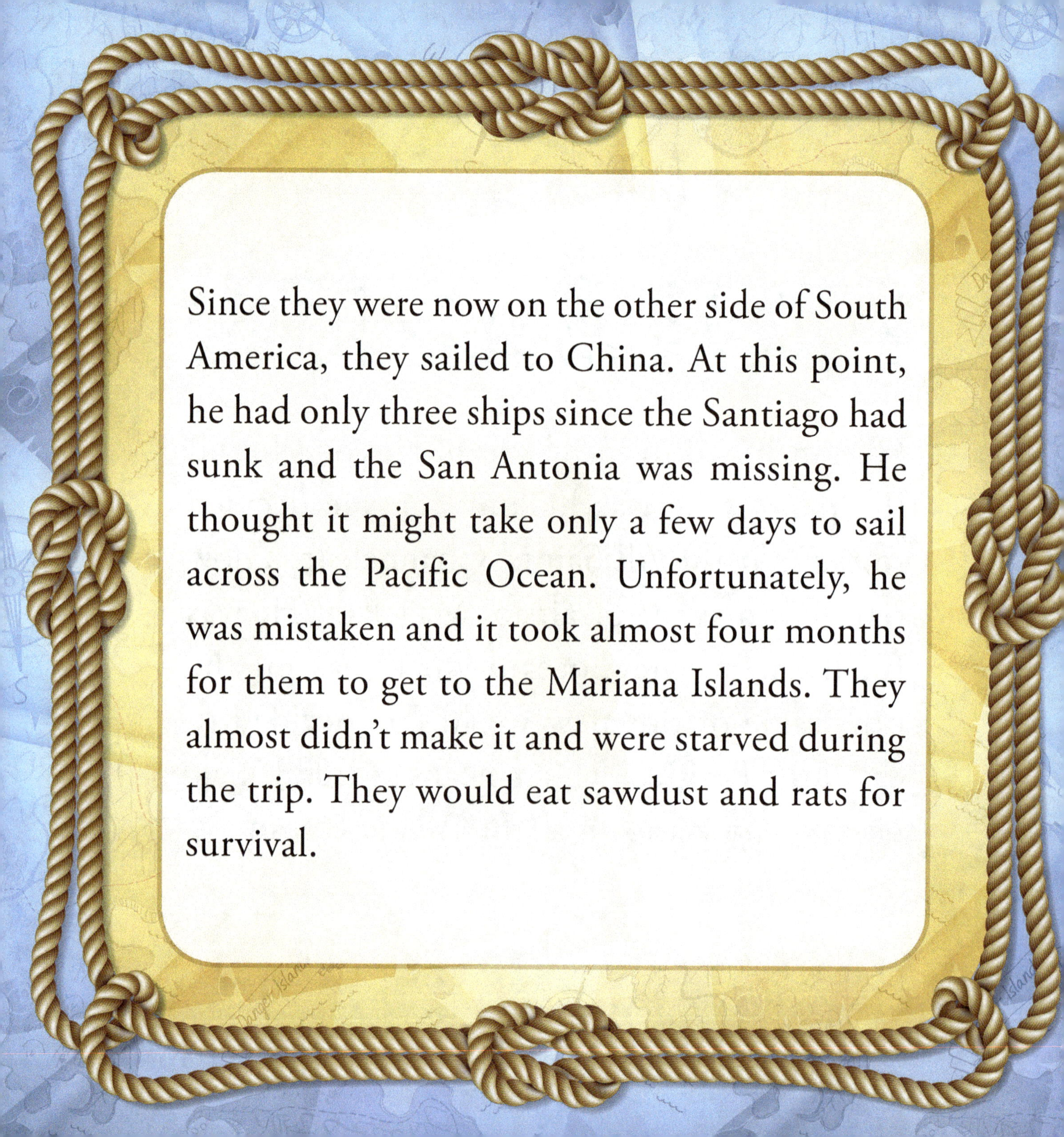

Since they were now on the other side of South America, they sailed to China. At this point, he had only three ships since the Santiago had sunk and the San Antonia was missing. He thought it might take only a few days to sail across the Pacific Ocean. Unfortunately, he was mistaken and it took almost four months for them to get to the Mariana Islands. They almost didn't make it and were starved during the trip. They would eat sawdust and rats for survival.

Mariana Islands

MADRIDEJOS
BANTAYAN
SANTA FE
DAANBANTAYAN
MEDELLIN
SAN REMIGIO
BOGO
TABOGON
TABUELAN
BORBON
SOGOD
TUBURAN
CATMON
PILAR
SAN FRANCISCO
PORO
TUDELA
ASTURIAS
CARMEN
DANAO
BALAMBAN
COMPOSTELA
LILOAN
CEBU CITY
TOLEDO
CONSOLACION
MANDAUE
MINGLANILLA
PINAMUNGAHAN
LAPU-LAPU
TALISAY
NAGA
CORDOVA
ALOGUINSAN
SAN FERNANDO
BARILI
CARCAR
DUMANJUG
SIBONGA
RONDA
ALCANTARA
MOALBOAL
ARGAO
BADIAN
DALAGUETE
ALEGRIA
ALCOY
MALABUYOC
BOLJOON
GINATILAN
SAMBOAN
OSLOB
SANTANDER

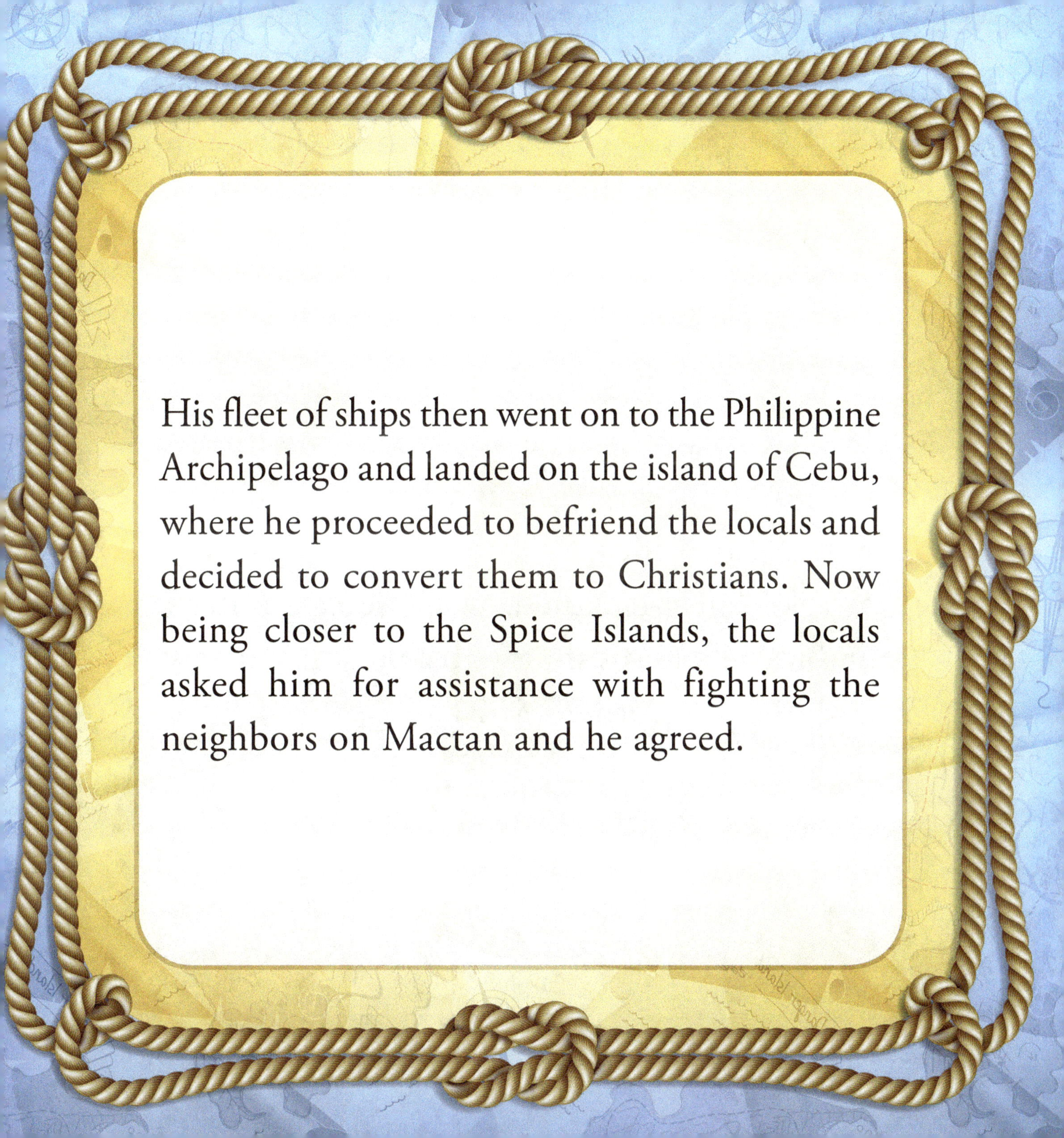

His fleet of ships then went on to the Philippine Archipelago and landed on the island of Cebu, where he proceeded to befriend the locals and decided to convert them to Christians. Now being closer to the Spice Islands, the locals asked him for assistance with fighting the neighbors on Mactan and he agreed.

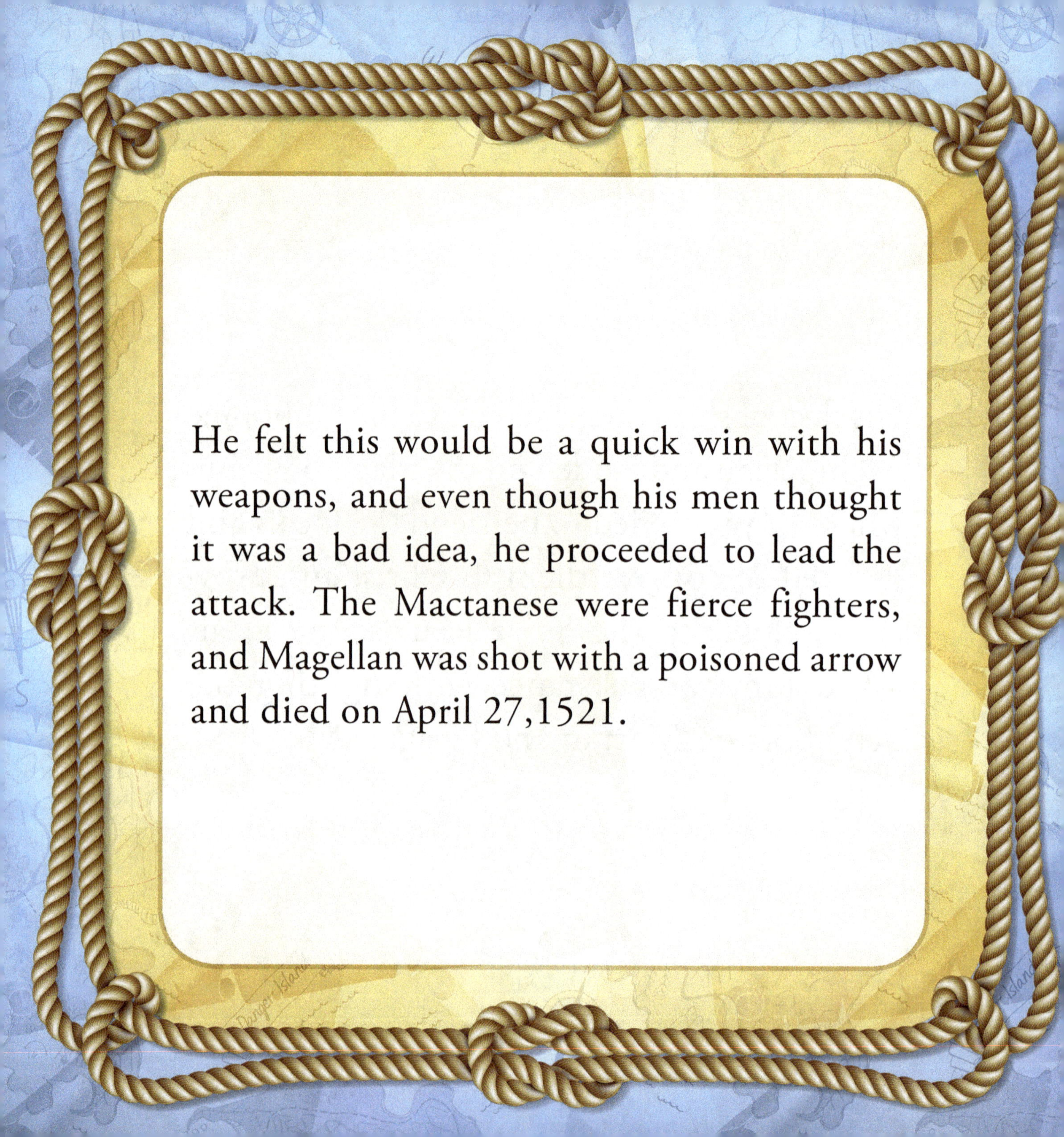

He felt this would be a quick win with his weapons, and even though his men thought it was a bad idea, he proceeded to lead the attack. The Mactanese were fierce fighters, and Magellan was shot with a poisoned arrow and died on April 27,1521.

Mactan Shrine

Moluccas

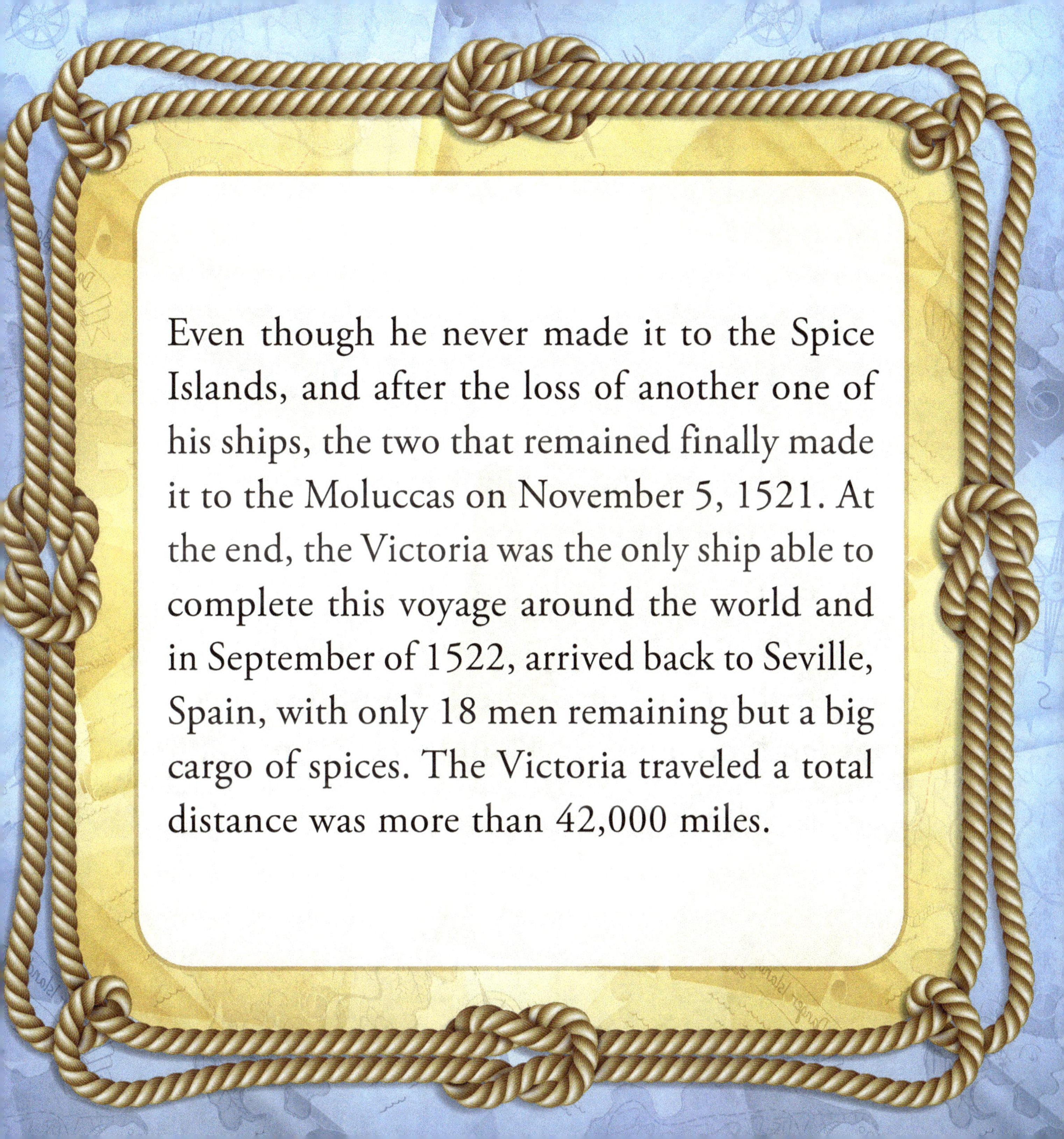

Even though he never made it to the Spice Islands, and after the loss of another one of his ships, the two that remained finally made it to the Moluccas on November 5, 1521. At the end, the Victoria was the only ship able to complete this voyage around the world and in September of 1522, arrived back to Seville, Spain, with only 18 men remaining but a big cargo of spices. The Victoria traveled a total distance was more than 42,000 miles.

MAGELLAN'S HISTORY

His ambitious and daring voyage to seek personal glory and riches gave the Europeans much more than merely spices. Even though his trip west to the east traveling the Strait of Magellan was mapped and discovered, it was too dangerous and too long to be a practical route to the Spice Islands.

Ferdinand Magellan

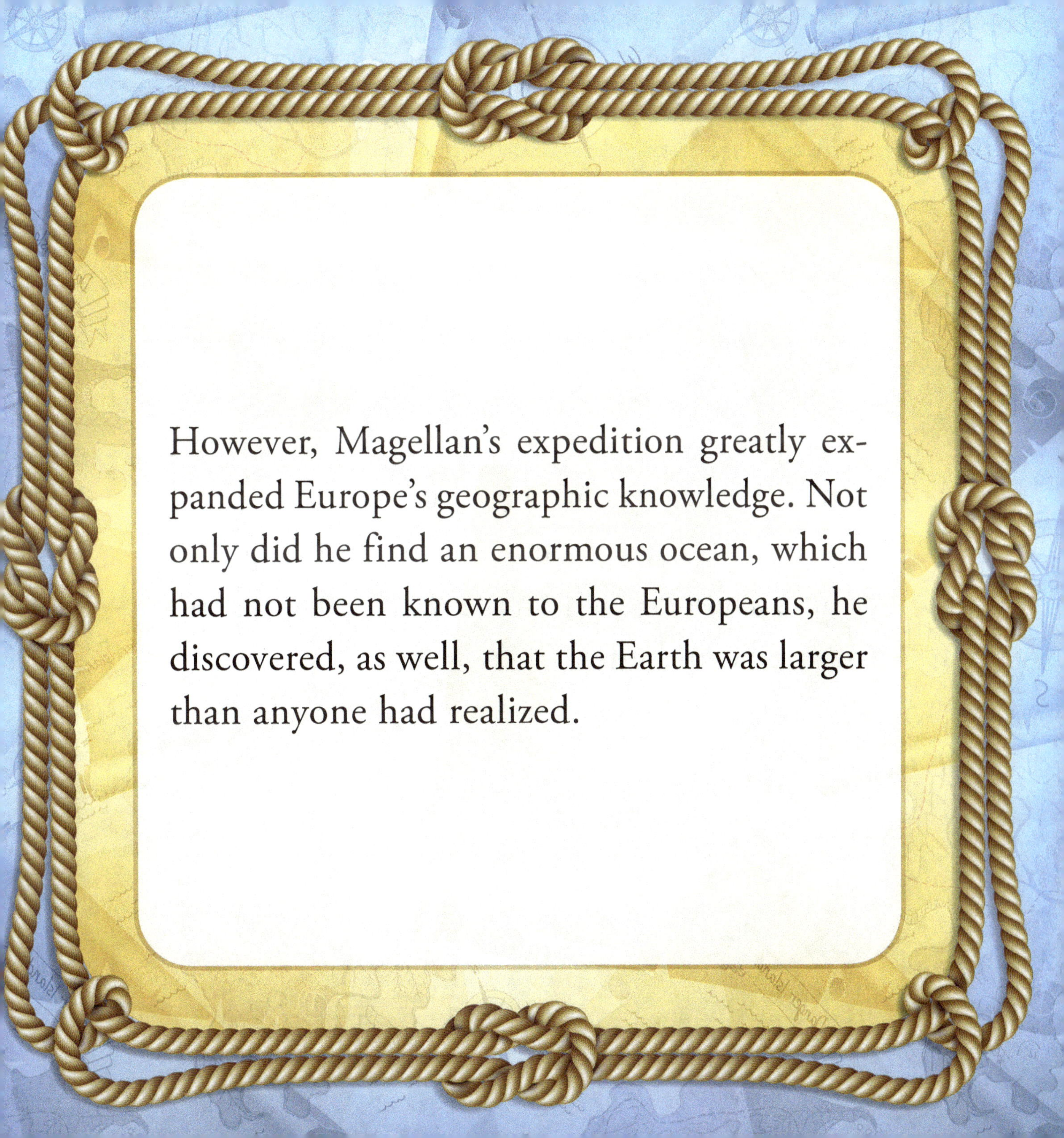

However, Magellan's expedition greatly expanded Europe's geographic knowledge. Not only did he find an enormous ocean, which had not been known to the Europeans, he discovered, as well, that the Earth was larger than anyone had realized.

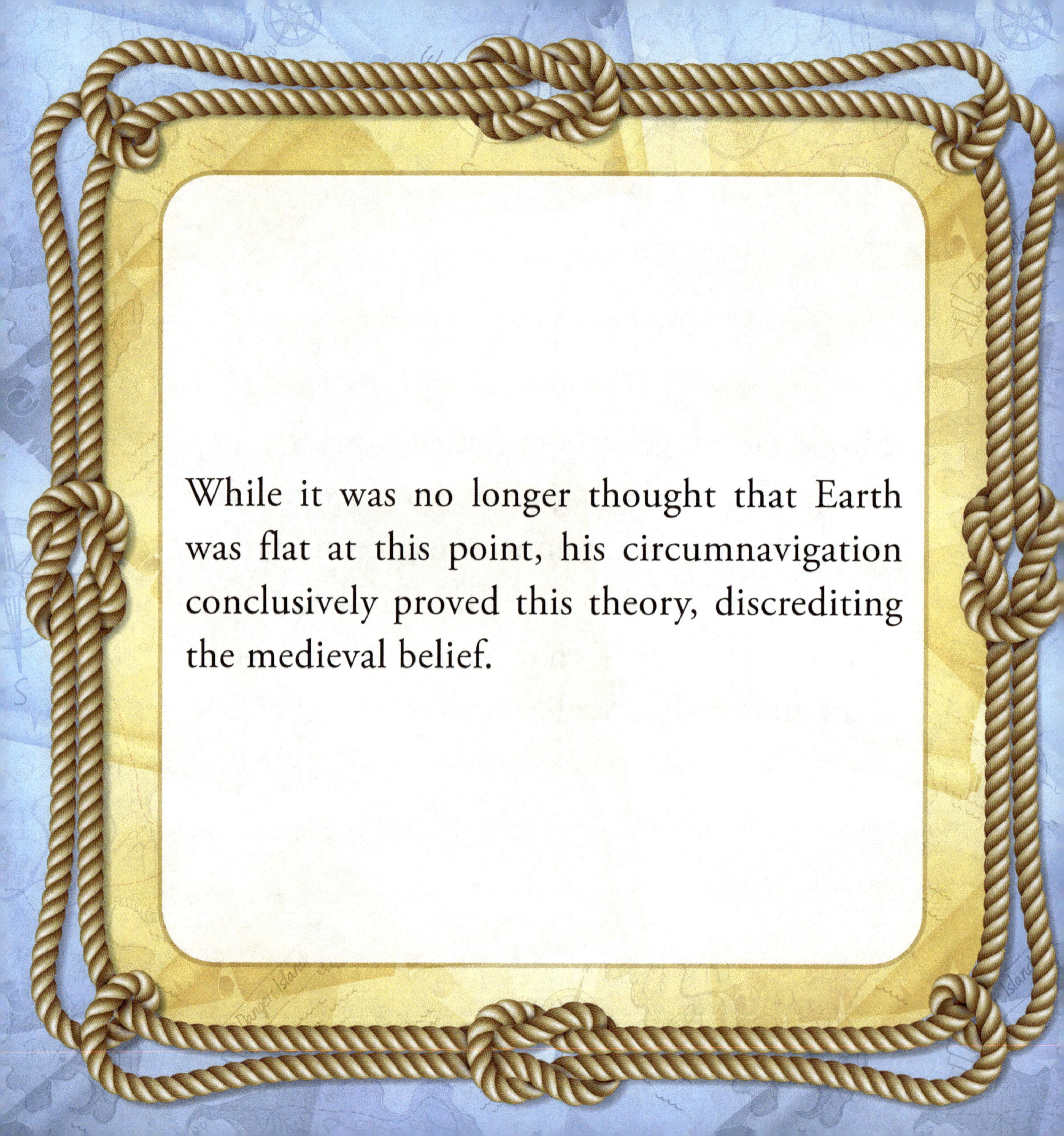

While it was no longer thought that Earth was flat at this point, his circumnavigation conclusively proved this theory, discrediting the medieval belief.

Map of the Philippines

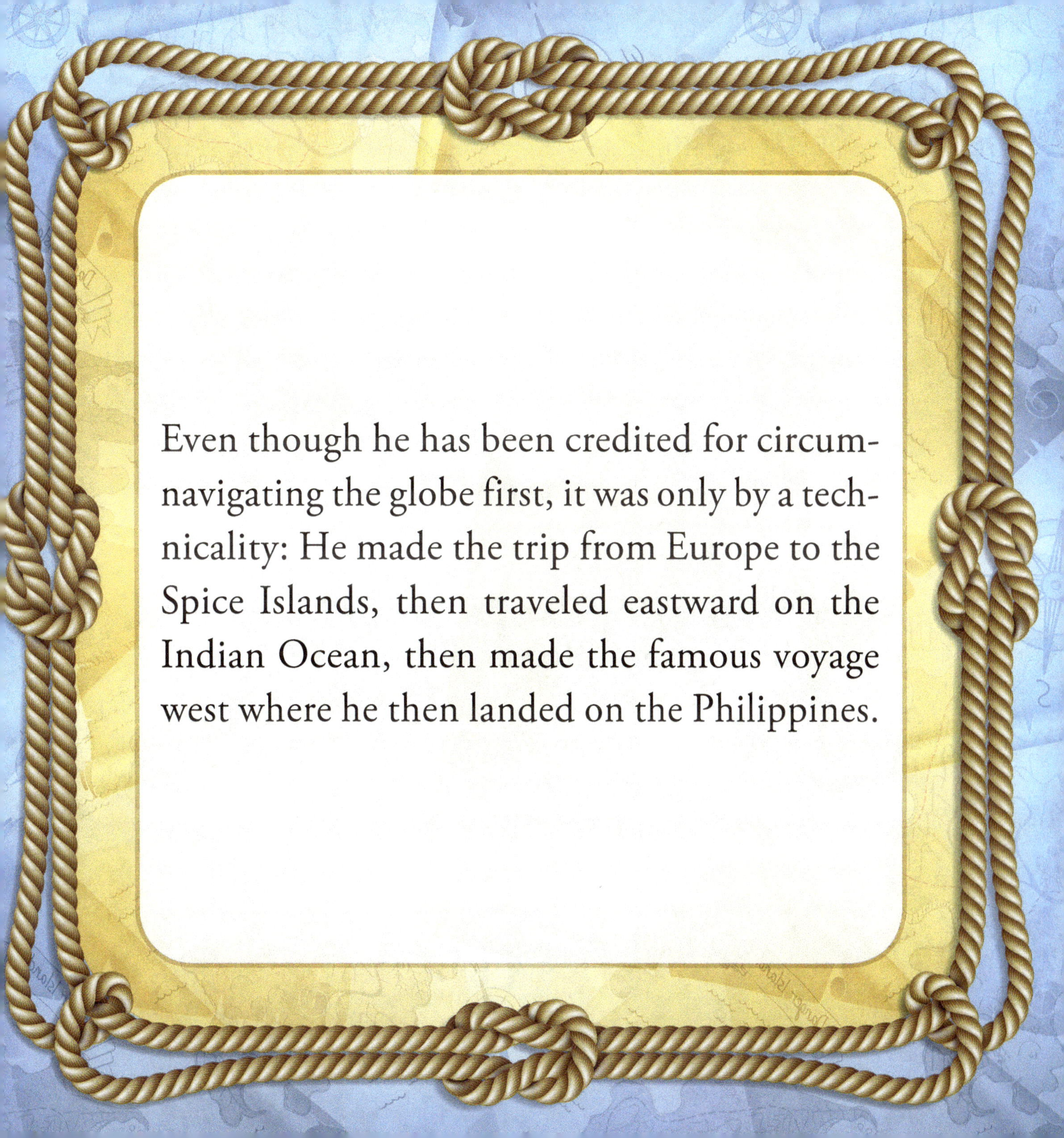

Even though he has been credited for circumnavigating the globe first, it was only by a technicality: He made the trip from Europe to the Spice Islands, then traveled eastward on the Indian Ocean, then made the famous voyage west where he then landed on the Philippines.

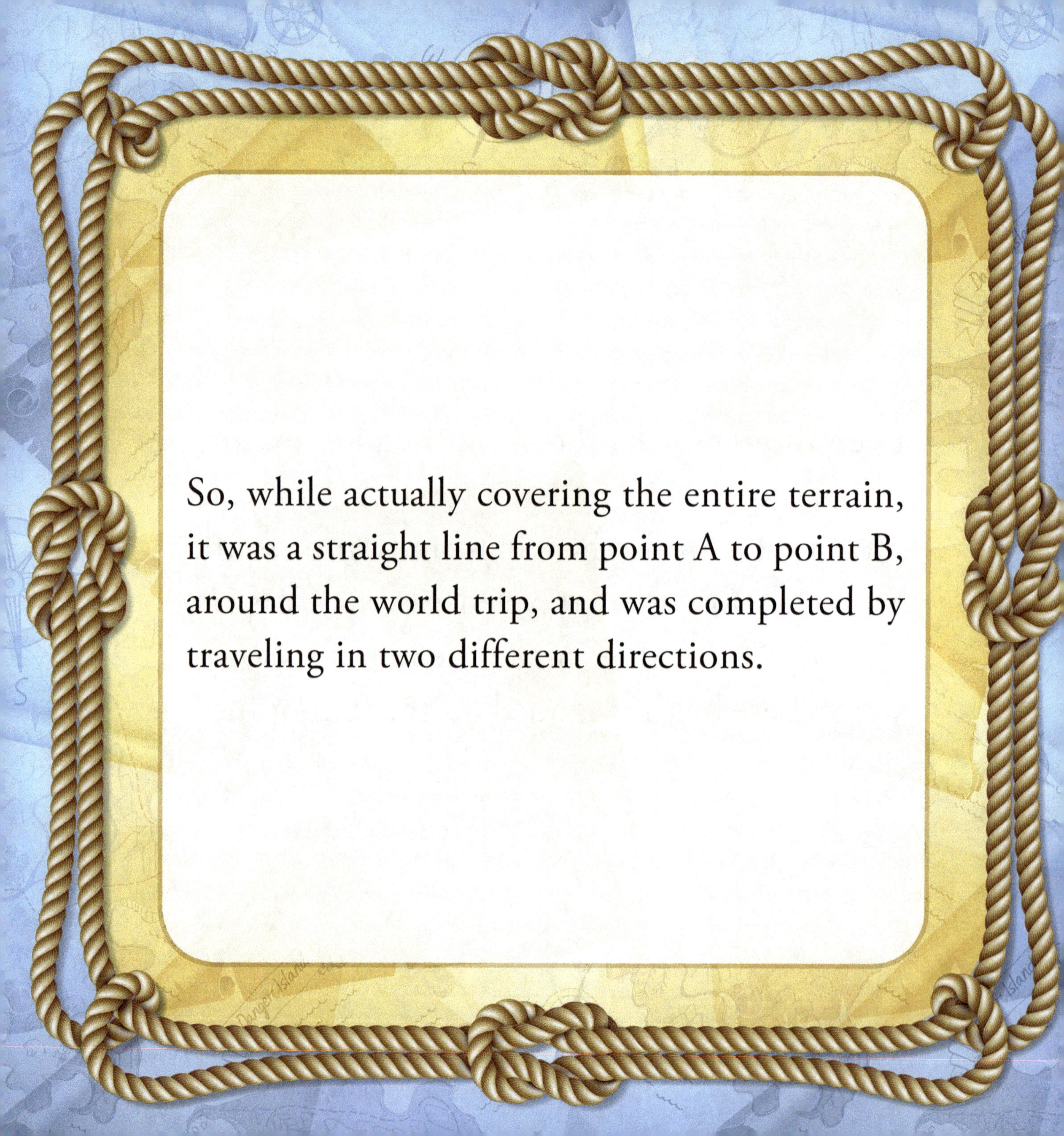

So, while actually covering the entire terrain, it was a straight line from point A to point B, around the world trip, and was completed by traveling in two different directions.

Prima ego velivolis ambivi cursibus Orbem,
Magellane novo te duce ducta freto.
Ambivi, meritoq; vocor VICTORIA: sunt mî
Vela, alæ; precium, gloria; pugna, mare.

Enrique of Mallaca

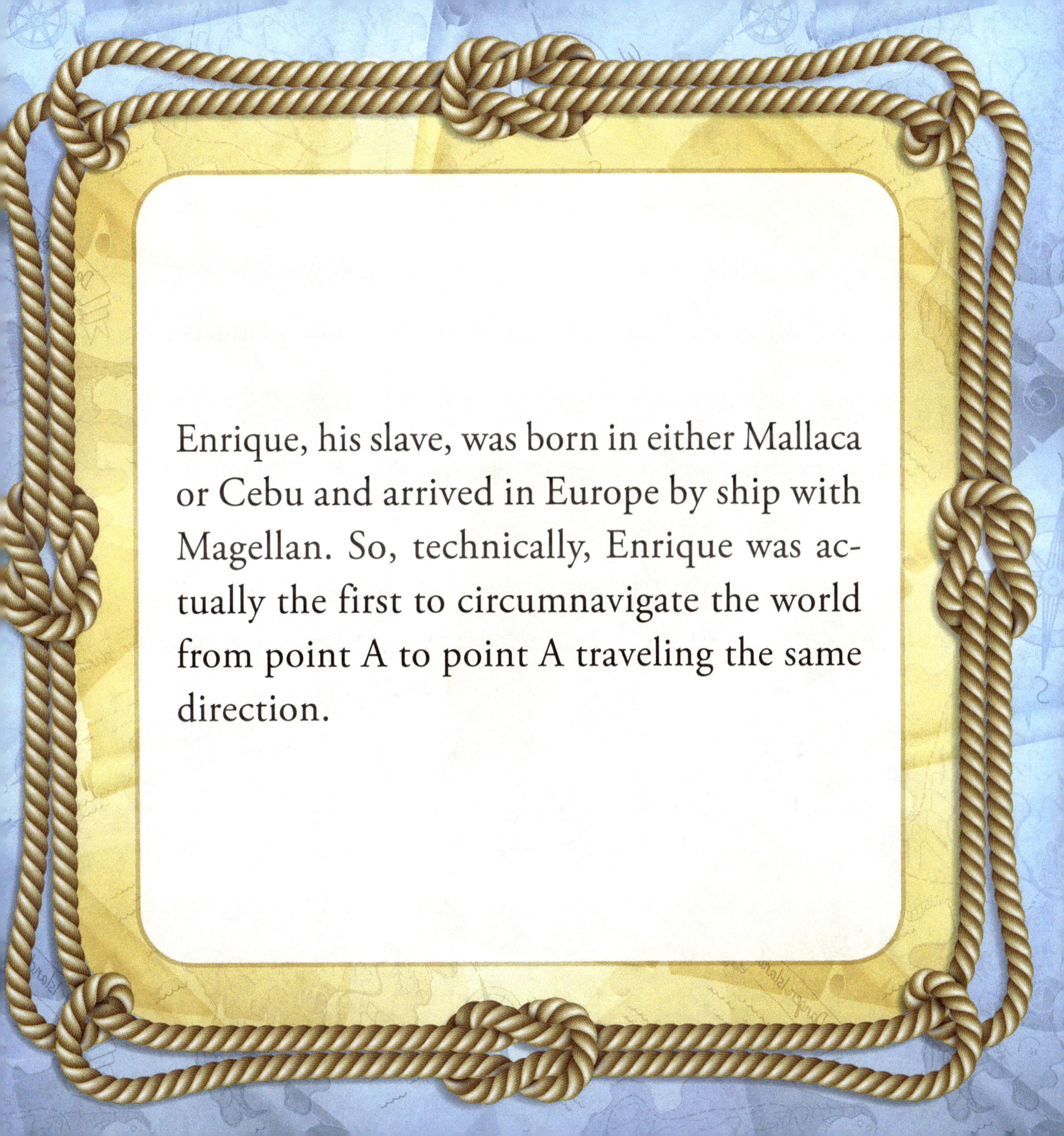

Enrique, his slave, was born in either Mallaca or Cebu and arrived in Europe by ship with Magellan. So, technically, Enrique was actually the first to circumnavigate the world from point A to point A traveling the same direction.

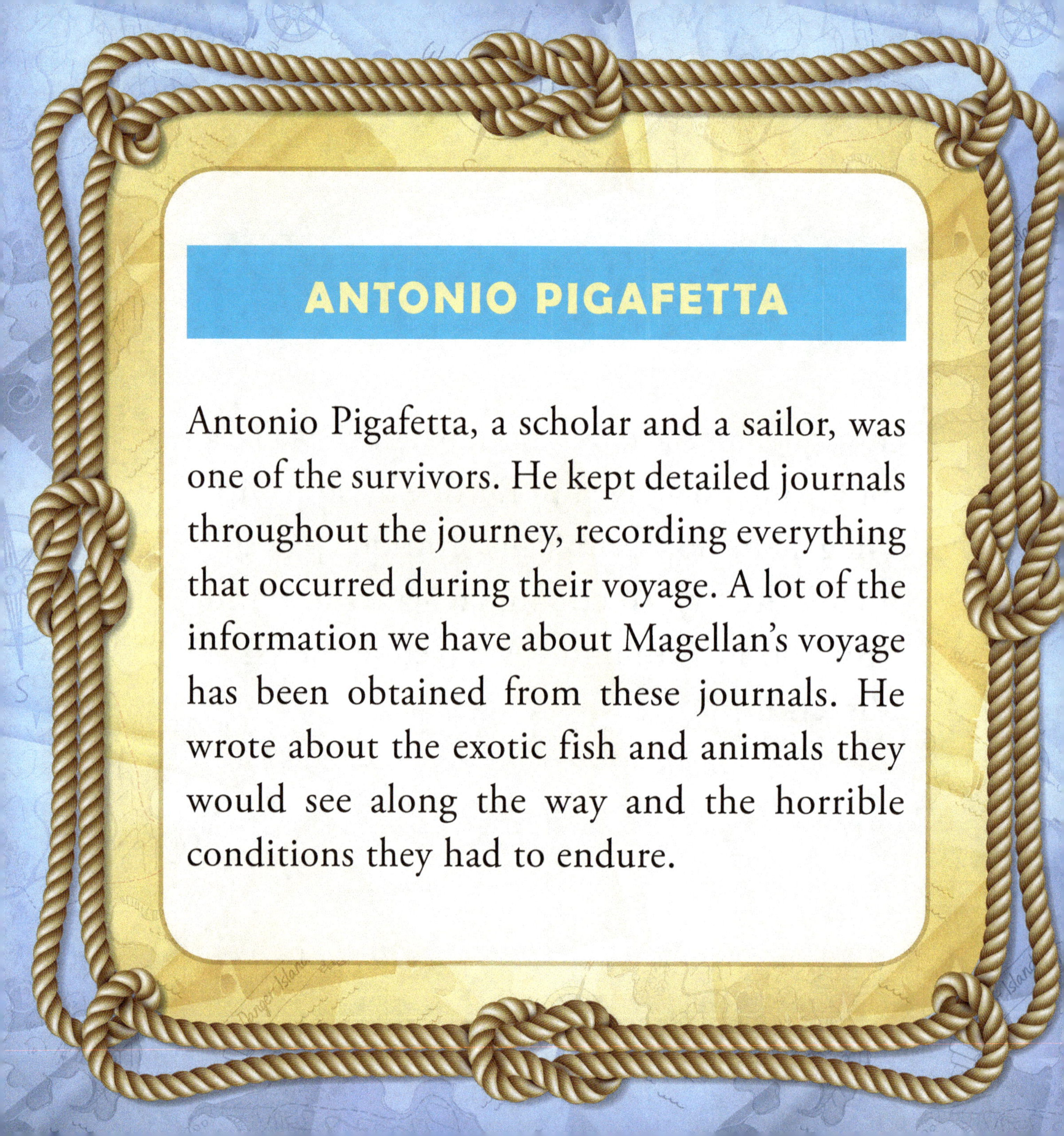

ANTONIO PIGAFETTA

Antonio Pigafetta, a scholar and a sailor, was one of the survivors. He kept detailed journals throughout the journey, recording everything that occurred during their voyage. A lot of the information we have about Magellan's voyage has been obtained from these journals. He wrote about the exotic fish and animals they would see along the way and the horrible conditions they had to endure.

Antonio Pigafetta

Ferdinand Magellan

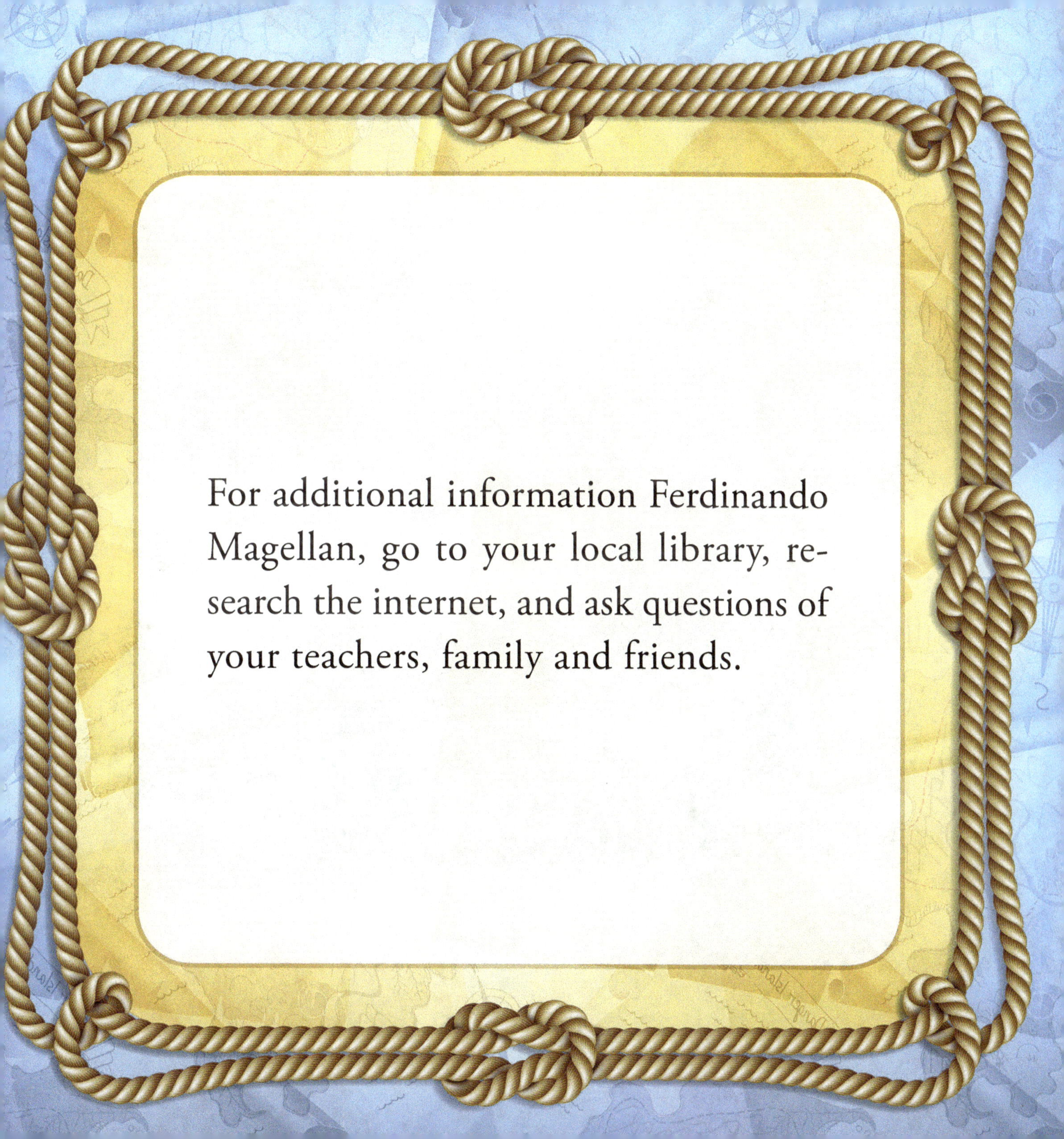

For additional information Ferdinando Magellan, go to your local library, research the internet, and ask questions of your teachers, family and friends.

Visit
BABY PROFESSOR
EDUCATION KIDS
www.BabyProfessorBooks.com
to download Free Baby Professor eBooks
and view our catalog of new and exciting
Children's Books

www.ingramcontent.com/pod-product-compliance
Lightning Source LLC
LaVergne TN
LVHW060828170826
845678LV00010B/1926
* 9 7 9 8 8 6 9 4 3 2 9 7 1 *